MW00903501

JESUS
OUR RIGHTEOUS HEALER
Vs.
CORONAVIRUS (COVID-19)

VICKIE L. HALL AND DARRYL J. HALL SR.

WESTBOW
PRESS®
A DIVISION OF THOMAS NELSON
& ZONDERVAN

WestBow Press books may be ordered through booksellers or by contacting:

WestBow Press
A Division of Thomas Nelson & Zondervan
1663 Liberty Drive
Bloomington, IN 47403
www.westbowpress.com
844-714-3454

Scripture quotations marked KJV are taken from the King James Version.

Scripture quotations marked NIV are taken from The Holy Bible, New International Version®, NIV® Copyright © 1973, 1978, 1984, 2011 by Biblica, Inc.® Used by permission. All rights reserved worldwide.

ISBN: 978-1-6642-0861-2 (sc)
ISBN: 978-1-6642-0860-5 (hc)
ISBN: 978-1-6642-0862-9 (e)

Library of Congress Control Number: 2020920075

Print information available on the last page.

WestBow Press rev. date: 11/12/2020

The Dedication

I first dedicate this book to Jesus Christ, my Lord and Savior, because He is the Author and the Finisher of my faith. Without Him, I would not be here today. He's the One who deserves all the honor, recognition, and glory, for it all belongs to Him.

This is also dedicated to our children, grandchildren, family, prayer warriors, medical professionals, the Body of Christ, and to everyone who is battling with the Coronavirus, other illnesses, trials, and tribulations.

A special dedication is for my husband, Darryl, for his love, support, commitment, and collaboration with me on this project.

The Introduction

This book is not a fairytale. Rather, it is about how God performed so many miracles for me. I am a real living testimony of how I overcame death many times.

It is a good thing to have a relationship with God. Why? Well, because from the beginning of Creation, God created Adam and Eve, and they became one flesh. Therefore, God loves family and union. Anything that is divided will not stand. Although we have relationships with our spouses/significant others, children, parents, and friends, we still need to have a relationship with Jesus.

There are benefits for God's people when we are one with Him. He has a living will, waiting for all who belong to Him. We are heirs to His Kingdom—His beneficiaries—from everlasting to everlasting.

"In my Father's house are many mansions; if it were not so,
I would have told you. I go to prepare a place for you."
~ John 14:2 ~ (KJV)

God is the ONLY Savior who can save your soul from a burning Hell. He protects us from the adversary whenever he tries to take us out with fiery darts. God is also the SAME GOD who heals us when we are sick in our body, which is why I call Him my Righteous Healer. He's the "I am that I am God"!

This book was written for anyone who needs a Savior, Counselor, and true Friend. Jesus is the answer to every problem, as He is a Problem-Solver. He is also a Heart-Fixer and a Mind-Regulator. His Word alone is God.

"In the beginning was the Word, and the Word was with God, and the Word was God."
~ John 1:1 ~ (KJV)

He is the answer for the world today and forever. We all need Him. It doesn't matter who you are or where you live, He knows your name. The very hairs on your head are all numbered. In God's eyes, ALL lives matter. He died on the Cross at Calvary for ALL humankind so that we may have life and have it more abundantly. God could not find anyone else to lay down their life for this world because no one else besides His Son, Jesus Christ, was worthy. It is because of God's love that He gave His Only Begotten Son to die as payment for our sinful nature.

We must be watchful and always pray (Matthew 26:41), for the time is near. We are living in the last days. When we are observant, we can see the signs all around us. Jesus is on His way back to lay claim to His people—those of us who are ready.

The devil is seeking whom he may devour. He knows his time is almost up. We can see his evil works taking place every day and everywhere in the land with all the killing, stealing, and destruction.

I encourage everyone who doesn't know Jesus for themselves to call on His name while He is near, for He will answer you. We can call on Jesus any time because His line is never busy.

"Behold, the Lord's hand is not shortened that it cannot save; neither His ear heavy that it cannot hear..."
~ Isaiah 59:1(a) ~ (KJV)

Table of Contents

Chapter One:

The Beginning

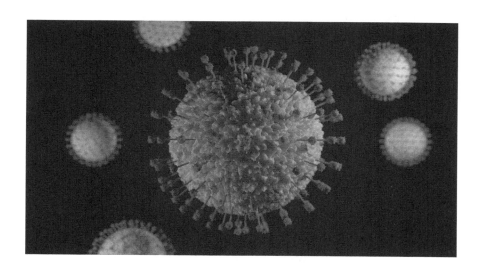

The date was early March 2020. My husband, Darryl, and I were on vacation and traveled to North Carolina to spend time with our children and grandchildren. We also went to Davis Station, South Carolina, to do the Lord's will and to be about our Father's business.

How many of you know that whenever you do good, evil is always present?

After spending time in South Carolina, we returned to our daughter's house in Dallas, North Carolina, on March 10th. That morning, I started feeling ill with fever and coughing. To add to it, my body was getting weak. At the time, I didn't think too much about it. I assumed it was "just a little bug in the air" and that the feelings would subside. Darryl went and purchased some over-the-counter medication for me, but nothing seemed to work. Each day that went by, I wasn't getting any better. In fact, my condition worsened drastically.

It was then my daughter said, "You need to go to the hospital."

"No," I told her. "Maybe by the end of the week, I will feel better."

I called my mother in Florida and explained to her how I was feeling. Immediately, she began praying with me over the phone. After prayer, she instructed me to go to the hospital to get checked out.

How many of you know that prayer changes things?

When I started craving fresh fruit, Darryl went to the store to buy some for me that Saturday morning. By the time he returned, my appetite had disappeared.

Later that afternoon, a family member called and had prayer with me. She then told me to get some natural herbs and other ingredients and boil them together to make a tea. Darryl went back to the store to purchase the items on the list. When he returned, he boiled the herbs and ingredients in the kitchen downstairs. I recall him telling me that when he returned, he heard me upstairs laughing and playing with our daughter and grandchildren, so he assumed I was feeling better. Shortly thereafter, my body began to feel ice cold. I laid down in the bed with four layers of blankets trying to get warm.

The strangest thing then happened: My two-year-old grandson and seven-year-old niece came into the room, sat next to me in the bed, and just stared at me. They would not move. It was as if they knew there was something that was seriously wrong with me. When my daughter walked back into the room, I asked her to bring me another blanket because my body was chilled to the bone.

Meanwhile, the Lord spoke to Darryl and told him to head upstairs to my side. By the time he arrived—my tea in his hand—my whole body had begun shutting down. My countenance had changed, my skin turned very dark, and my breathing was very shallow. Instantly, he was alarmed.

You see, my husband had just retired after serving almost

28 years in law enforcement. He said he had seen "that look" many times before. It was the look of death.

As he looked upon me, the concern evident in his voice, he exclaimed, "What in the WORLD"

"I need to go to the hospital," I replied.

"Are you okay?!" The concern grew even more intense. I was too weak to reply. He then tried to pick me up, but my body was like dead weight. Lifting me was proving exceedingly difficult. He asked the children to leave the room, but they didn't move. The second time he asked them was done with a louder, more commanding tone. We were in desperate times. Life was literally leaving my body, and he did not want them to bear witness to my impending death.

Hearing all the commotion, my daughter hurriedly returned to the bedroom with the fifth blanket I had requested earlier. Darryl told her to call the ambulance, which she did immediately.

In an effort to open an airway so that my breathing would improve, Darryl wedged his body between the headboard and my back, pushing me up to force me into an almost upright position. In my ear, he repeatedly whispered, "Keep breathing," and prayed over me that I remained alive until the Emergency Medical Technicians (EMTs) arrived.

As soon as the EMTs came into the room, they did their routine checks of my vitals and temperature. It turned out I had a very high fever. They also gave me oxygen to assist me with breathing. A second set of EMTs arrived shortly after, and they continued working on me, trying to get my breathing under control. Although my temperature was high, my body remained ice cold. The blankets were removed in hopes that my temperature would go down. Immediately, my body began to shake uncontrollably with chills.

Once they got me downstairs and into one of the ambulances, I was rushed to a local area hospital Emergency Room (ER) while my husband followed in the car.

You might be wondering why he didn't ride with me. The answer is simple: He had to retrieve our Bibles first, and the EMTs couldn't wait. We never travel without the Word of God. We even sleep with it in our bed, sometimes under our pillows.

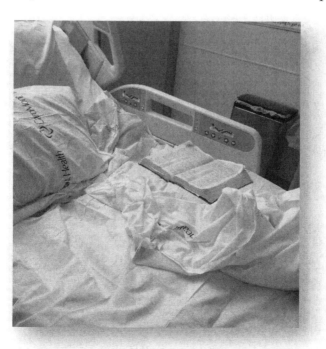

Image 1 of Vickie's Bible in the bed…as usual.
Photograph taken by Darryl Hall, Sr.

When we arrived at the hospital's ER, I was immediately placed in a room with Darryl by my side, and they began to run tests on me. By that time, my countenance had returned—likely due to the oxygen and intravenous fluids that were administered.

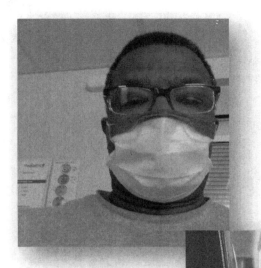

Selfie of Darry Hall, Sr.

Image 2, and 3 of one of many Medications administered.

As we waited for the results of the testing, it was then we learned about COVID-19—the Coronavirus. When the doctor came in to inform us about the test results, he said, "You don't have the Coronavirus, based on the CDC's (Center Of Disease Control's) criteria, but you do have pneumonia in your right lung."

I was very shocked by that diagnosis. I didn't feel like I had pneumonia. Instead, it felt like I had a cold or some other common condition that wouldn't go away.

From that point, everything started going downhill for me. I was admitted and assigned to a room. I was told to expect to be in the hospital for at least three days for treatment and that I would be sent home with medication.

I began to pray a silent prayer.

Chapter Two:

The Process

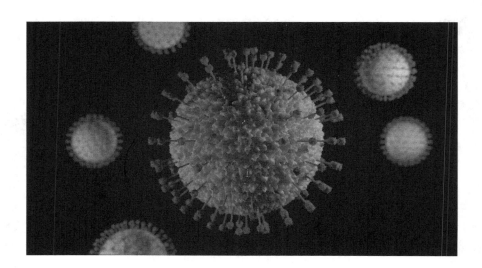

Initially, treatment consisted of a regimen of antibiotics for pneumonia and hospital-grade Tylenol for the high fever. Every time the Tylenol was administered, my temperature would go down, but once it wore off, the fever returned. The doctors could not figure out why the medicine wasn't working, so they ran more tests.

By that time, I had three doctors assigned to my case: an infectious disease doctor, a pulmonologist (lung doctor), and the attending physician. It's important to note here that each doctor prescribed medications based on what each thought was wrong with me.

The infectious disease doctor was treating me for viral and bacterial infections.

The pulmonologist was treating me for my lung deficiency.

The attending physician was treating me for the flu (Influenza) and fever.

During my stay, I was given another COVID-19 test. We all waited anxiously for the results so that proper treatment for whatever ailed me could begin. Mind you, Darryl remained in the room with me unguarded since my arrival…While we waited for the results of the COVID-19 test, more chest x-rays and bloodwork were ordered. The infectious disease doctor said he was really concerned about my fever and that he suspected I did, indeed, have the virus.

"I do NOT have the Coronavirus," I stated matter-of-factly.

Darryl also replied. "If she has Coronavirus, then I have it, too, because I have been with her everywhere! We traveled together in the same car for the past several months, stayed in hotels together, and shared meals, including eating and drinking after each other. I know she doesn't have it because I don't have it!"

As the days passed by, my prognosis continued to worsen. Initially, I only had pneumonia in my right lung. It then spread to both. The doctors started treating me for Lupus Disease because my body started retaining water.

No matter what we heard, Darryl and I continued to pray and kept believing in God's Word. (Psalms 139 :13) (KJV) says that God formed my inward parts. Not only am I God's masterpiece, but He has a special plan for me. My existence is no mistake. We know the doctors have book knowledge and are experts in their specific fields, BUT GOD has all power in HIS hands. It was time to call on our Prayer Warriors.

Darryl and I are part of a prayer line that was established in Miami, Florida, 15 years ago. It is called "Miracle Temple Prayer Line Lifeline." My mother was entrusted with that assignment by God. Well, the Prayer Warriors fell on their knees and cried out to God for a miracle on my behalf. How many know that prayer is our secret weapon.

How many of you know that sometimes, things have to get worse before they can get better?

At that point, everything was chaotic and out of whack.

Darryl and I were placed in and out of isolation repeatedly, all because the doctors could not determine what was really going on with the fever that was attacking my body. In fact, the fever would be so high, the medication they were treating me with no longer worked effectively. The nurses grew worried, and more doctors came to see me, as well. A decision had to be made concerning my condition, so we were ordered back into isolation.

The attending physician had me tested again for COVID-19— and the results came back positive. It's important to note that during this early process, I was tested SEVEN TIMES for the virus. I was confused and could not believe what I heard. I never thought the Coronavirus would have attack me. How in the world did I come in contact with it? Honestly, I hadn't heard of it until we arrived at the hospital. Needless to say, I was shocked and caught by surprise.

When it was confirmed that I had COVID-19, it felt surreal… like I was in a dream. Despite what my ears heard concerning the doctor's report, I had to keep my eyes on the prize: Jesus Christ, my Righteous Healer. I had to believe the LORD'S report, no matter what the doctors were saying.

"Who hath believed our report?
And to whom is the arm of the Lord revealed?"
~ Isaiah 53:1 ~(KJV)

I repeatedly reminded myself to keep the faith, knowing that God can do anything. I know the God I served and lived for has all power over my body and every sickness and disease.

Still, in all my humanness, my body grew weaker. I was losing my appetite, and my oxygen level started to drop dangerously low. As my vitals continued to fail, I felt my body shutting down. No matter what kind of medication they treated me with, nothing worked. My faith in God, however, never faltered.

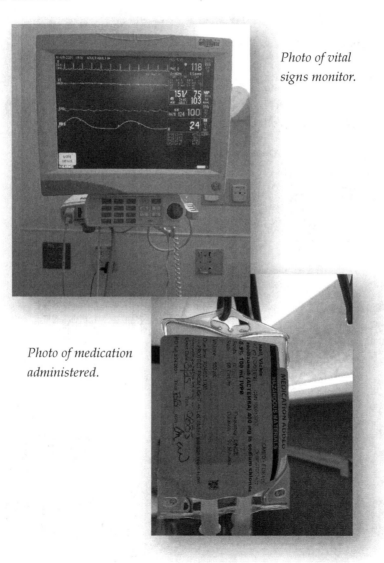

Photo of vital signs monitor.

Photo of medication administered.

Chapter Three:

The Favor with God and Favor with Man

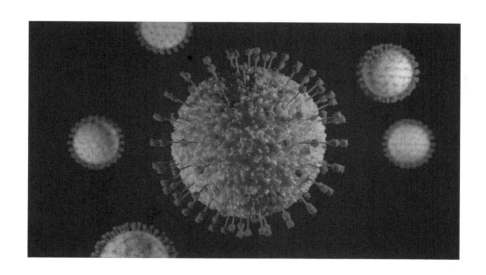

During the whole process, my hospital stay extended from an estimated three (initially) to 30 days. Favor with God and man were with us.

"Then you will win favor and a good name
in the sight of God and man."
~ Proverbs 3:4 ~(NIV)

In the beginning stages of my diagnosis and treatments, Darryl was allowed to stay with me for approximately two weeks—even with the doctors suspecting I had COVID-19. Once it was determined I was positive for the virus, they told him he could no longer stay because of the CDC's protocol and guidelines that stated (summarily):

"COVID-19 PATIENTS ARE NOT ALLOWED TO HAVE ANY VISITORS AND MUST BE ISOLATED...ALONE."

Darryl told the hospital staff he was not leaving me there alone because he didn't want to hear later on that something went wrong. They kept insisting he couldn't stay.

Although in a weakened state, I found the strength to tell them, "If my husband cannot stay with me, I will sign myself out and go to another hospital." I was unmovable on that stance because, after all, he and I agreed that since we came in together, we would be leaving together. The staff went and spoke with the hospital's Administrator, who said that if Darryl stayed, he would have to be isolated with me and could not leave the facility. Darryl agreed to those terms. They further stated that if he started showing symptoms, he would have to be taken to a tent on the outside grounds to be tested for the virus and not be permitted to return to isolation with me.

As time progressed, my condition continued to deteriorate, yet Darryl never showed any symptoms. In fact, the Attending Physician gave him a thermometer to check his own temperature daily. Had he developed a high fever, he was to notify the staff immediately. Every day, his temperature was below normal. The nurses and doctors were amazed that Darryl had no symptoms or developed any signs of the virus during his entire stay, even while being in isolation with me. The staff often came to the room, asking him if he had a fever or was experiencing a cough. Many thought he should have been tested regardless of how he felt.

"They don't need to fear me; they need to fear God," he used to say.

As time went by, God proved Himself. We later learned via television media outlets and social media that people were dropping off their family members and loved ones to the ER once they even suspected someone was virus-laden. Those family members were placed into isolation…alone. We personally know of no other person who was allowed to stay in isolation with their loved ones after being diagnosed with Coronavirus. Sadly, many of those cases resulted in people succumbing to the disease.

We count it a blessing for Darryl to have been permitted to remain in isolation with me for the entirety of my 30-day stay as I battled COVID-19. Without a shadow of a doubt, we knew God's favor was with us.

> *"What shall we then say to these things?*
> *If God be for us, who can be against us?"*
> **~ Romans 8:31 ~(KJV)**

With that said, you must keep in mind that Darryl staying with me went against the CDC's guidelines, as well as the hospital's regulations, yet the favor of man was with us. The staff individually provided my husband with food, clothing, and personal hygiene items during the whole 30-day period.

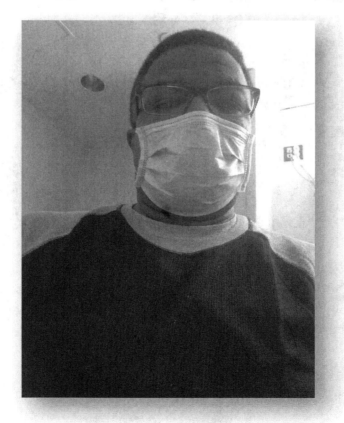

Selfie of Darryl Hall, Sr. Image 6

We are very grateful for the favor with God and man. Whenever you keep your trust in God, He will make a way for you. No matter what we may have to endure, God is still in charge. He is Omnipotent, meaning He has all power —and His power is unlimited. He can do anything He wants to do!

"Let the favor of the Lord our God be upon us; and establish the work of our hands upon us; yes, establish the work of our hands!"
~ Psalm 90:17 ~(ESV)

I will shout it to the world anytime and anywhere:

GOD'S FAVOR IS WHAT GOT US TO THIS POINT! WE WOULD HAVE NEVER MADE IT WITHOUT HIS FAVOR!

Chapter Four:

The Turning Point

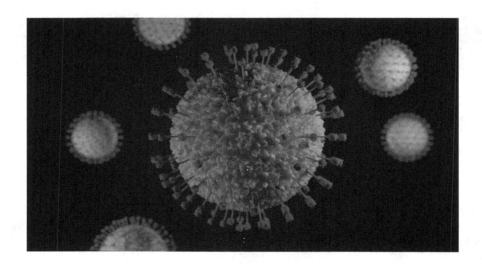

As I stated before, my body was shutting down, primarily due to the lack of food intake, which, after the first week, was virtually non-existent. Darryl kept telling me, "Baby, if you don't eat or drink, you're not going to be able to survive." The machines that monitored my vital signs and oxygen levels started to sound their alarms more frequently, indicating my life was slowly leaving my body.

"The thief cometh not but for to steal, to kill, and to destroy.
I am come that they might have life,
and that they night have it more abundantly."
~ John 10:10 ~(KJV)

At one point, the doctors spoke to Darryl about placing me on the ventilator because time was running out, but he told them no because he wanted to respect my wishes—the ones we discussed at home before COVID-19. I told him I did not want to be on a ventilator because, through the years, I have experienced loved ones whose bodies break down while on those machines. When he had that conversation, I was in a deep sleep and could feel death looming. However, for whatever reason, I opened my eyes and saw my husband and the doctor talking. I could tell the doctor was vehemently trying to convince my husband to agree to have me placed on a ventilator. Darryl stood firm and told him, "No, use other alternatives, or do whatever process is next!"

"By the time we do all of that, it may well be too late to save her," came the response.

I called Darryl over to me and told him I wanted to speak with him.

The doctor then said, "Okay. I will leave and let the two of you talk."

"No. Don't leave. In fact, you need to hear what I have to say," I said weakly. I then told my husband, "I want to go on the ventilator." To say he was surprised is an understatement. As quiet as it's kept, I was surprised, too!

How many of you know that God will use the foolish things to confound the wise?

As I finished speaking, I could feel the coldness overcoming my body. I just knew the time was near and that my soul was preparing to leave my physical body.

"Are you sure?" the doctor asked.

"Yes! Is going on the ventilator going to help save my life?"

"Possibly. It at least gives you a chance," he said with a level of confidence he knew from science and his studies. He immediately went to retrieve his staff to prepare me for the ventilator.

As I laid on the bed, I began to trust God even more. I didn't know how He was going to do it. Neither did I know how I was going to come through it. With Darryl by my side and the doctors and nurses surrounding me, everyone introduced themselves and explained to me everything concerning the procedure. I turned to my husband and said, "Before they start, please pray with them." He asked everyone to hold hands and bow their heads while he prayed. When he finished praying, I looked at each person individually before saying, "Okay. I am ready." I reminded Darryl to place my Bible under my pillow after they finished connecting me to the machine.

Not long after they began the process of connecting me to that life-saving machine, I closed my eyes and immediately fell into a coma. Darryl then contacted the Prayer Warriors to solicit their fervent prayers.

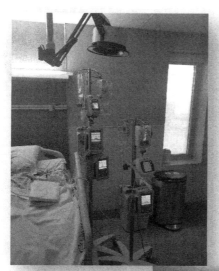

Photo of IV poles and medication pumps.

Photo of Vickie on the ventilator.

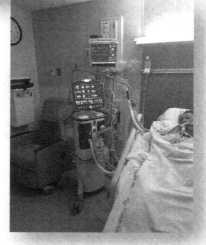

I was on the ventilator for eight days. According to the report from my husband, those days were full of much prayer, tears, and uncertainty. Long and restless days and nights seemed to blend into one. Darryl shared with me he experienced a rollercoaster ride of emotions as my vitals went up and down. Daily, they were either adding or subtracting medications. For every dose they gave me, he was right there, praying over it. He also Googled each so that he would know their purpose and side effects.

"My people are destroyed for lack of knowledge."
~ Hosea 4:6 ~(KJV)

We must always know what it is we are putting into our temple (body).

Chapter Five:

The Prayer Warriors

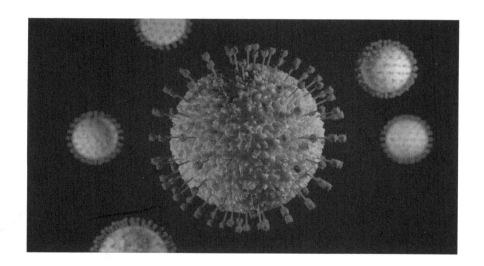

E arlier, I mentioned that the Miracle Temple Prayer Line Lifeline was established 15 years ago in Miami, Florida, and that my mother was entrusted with overseeing it. When God ordered her to institute that prayer line, she was obedient.

I cannot begin to count the number of times the Prayer Warriors have been called upon to fast and pray. Although we pray daily on the prayer line, some situations sometimes call for deeper penetration through spiritual and inspirational prayer. Throughout the years, many miracles have been performed and manifested by God on account of the Prayer Warriors.

I recall when I first called my mother when I went into the hospital, and the first thing she said was, "Okay. Let me call the Prayer Warriors and other saints."

> *"Is any sick among you? Let him call for the elders of the church, and let them pray over him, anointing him with oil in the name of the Lord; and the prayer of faith shall save the sick, and the Lord shall raise him up; and if he have committed sins, they shall be forgiven him. Confess your faults one to another, and pray for one another, that ye may be healed. The effectual fervent prayer of a righteous man availeth much."*
> **~ James 5:14-16 ~(KJV)**

My mother called the Elders, Bishops, Apostles, Pastors, and, of course, the Prayer Warriors. Everyone she called was praying for me. Some things only come through fasting and praying, and the Prayer Warriors prayed for me around the clock for 30 days. Believe it or not, they also prayed every three hours over the telephone with Darryl while I was on the ventilator. Whether I was conscious or not, he would place the phone near my ear. You see, he wanted me to get the prayers of the righteous in my spirit. In addition, he played gospel music in my room 24 hours a day so that I could also keep that in my spirit.

Darryl told me that one time, our Chief Apostle called from South Carolina and asked him to place the telephone on my chest as she prayed for me. He said that once she finished praying, she promised him I would not die and that God would raise me up. Another time, my mother called my husband and told him God spoke to her and said I would be coming out.

Day in and day out, Darryl spoke in my ear so that I knew he had not left me and remained by my side.

Prayers went up for me from multiples states, including:

- ❖ Florida (Thank You!)
- ❖ Georgia (Thank You!)
- ❖ South Carolina (Thank You!)
- ❖ North Carolina (Thank You!)
- ❖ Maryland (Thank You!)
- ❖ New York (Thank You!)
- ❖ Nevada (Thank You!) and
- ❖ Louisiana (Thank You!)

I thank God for all the prophecies, prayers, and words of encouragement that came forth.

Let me share something of great significance with you:

At precisely the same time three years prior to me falling ill, Darryl was sick and in a hospital in Miami with double-pneumonia. His prognosis was not good. The Prayer Warriors and Elders came together for him, and I was there by his side. He was in the hospital for three weeks, fighting for his life. The doctors had basically given up on him and just knew he was going to die. I remember it being a Thursday, and they said he would be dead by Monday. When they said he needed surgery and that the survival rate was 20%, I told them, "You are NOT God! We are believing in HIM to perform a miracle!" Needless to say, Darryl lived to have the surgery—on the same Monday the doctors said he would be dead by.

During the surgery, ten percent of his right lung was removed because the antibiotics were no longer working effectively. He was also told that because of the partial lung loss, he would be oxygen-dependent for the rest of his life.

Are you ready for the glory of God report?

Once Darryl was discharged from the hospital, he has NEVER used oxygen! He is completely healed!

I shared that here with you so that you not only understand the depths of God's power, but also so that you know why Darryl kept reminding me of how he experienced a similar health challenge and survived—although it wasn't COVID-19 that he had to contend with. Surely, if God brought him out and healed him, He would do the same for me!

I recall nights before I went on the ventilator, I struggled to breathe. When Darryl began to pray to God, he told Him, "I am going to walk the floor all night long until You show up in the room and allow Vickie's lungs to breathe." Not even ten minutes later, the numbers on the monitors began to increase, indicating I had stopped struggling to breathe. The next day, my numbers started decreasing again. Usually, when the monitors sounded an alarm, he called the Prayer Warriors, and they answered the call to get on bended knee and lift me in prayer. They prayed, and my oxygen levels improved—EVERY time.

Once I was placed on the ventilator, the struggle changed from me breathing to me surviving. Although the machine was breathing for me, my vitals were failing.

Darryl told me during that time, the Prayer Warriors sacrificed food and sleep as they fell on their faces before God, asking for a miracle. As I fought for my life, they continued praying, and God continued giving prophecy and revelation through them.

When I was removed from the ventilator, the spirit of uncertainty and depression reared its ugly head. I had no control over my body as it was being ravaged by the disease. I looked upon myself, and the tears rolled down my face. I am grateful for the Prayer Warriors who sung gospel songs to me to uplift my spirit and for the prayers for my mind, body, and soul. They also prayed for my husband's strength.

I thank God for my mother, who called daily and encouraged me not to give up and hold on to God's powerful hands. Not a day went by that she didn't call to check on Darryl and me. I really appreciate the love and bond he and I share. Only God and prayer could have allowed my husband and me to come out of isolation with a sound mind.

After 30 days at my hospital bedside, Darryl said he was conditioned to the sound of the alarms. Every time he heard one, he would automatically begin to pray.

While in the Critical Care Unit, we frequently heard ventilators sounding in the other patients' rooms, and we would pray for them.

My husband told me the Prayer Warriors gave him Psalm 91:1-16) (KJV)—also known as Jesus' 9-1-1—to read daily over me. It reads as follows:

"He that dwelleth in the secret place of the Most High shall abide under the shadow of the Almighty. I will say of the Lord, He is my refuge and my fortress: my God, in Him will I trust. Surely, He shall deliver thee from the snare of the fowler, and from the noisome pestilence. He shall cover thee with His feathers, and under His wings shalt thou trust: His truth shall be thy shield and buckler. Thou shall not be afraid for the terror by night; nor for the arrow that flieth by day; nor for the pestilence that walketh in darkness; nor for the destruction that wasteth at noonday. A thousand shall fall at thy side, and ten thousand at thy right hand; but it shall not come nigh thee. Only with thine eyes shalt thou behold and see the reward of the wicked. Because thou hast made the Lord, which is my refuge, even the Most High, thy habitation; there shall be no evil befall thee, neither shall any plague come nigh thy dwelling.

For He shall give His angels charge over thee, to keep thee in all thy ways. They shall bear thee up in their hands, lest thou dash thy foot against a stone. Thou shalt tread upon the lion and adder: the young lion and the dragon shalt thou trample under feet. Because He hath set His love upon me, therefore will I deliver Him: I will set Him on high, because He hath known My name. He shall call upon Me, and I will answer him: I will be with him in trouble; I will deliver him, and honour him. With long life will I satisfy him and shew him My salvation."

Much prayer = Much power!

How awesome is God? He knew 15 years ago that we—the Prayer Warriors—would need the Miracle Temple Prayer Line Lifeline for such a time as these. That's why He established it!

He KNOWS all, SEES all, and IS our All and All!

Miracle Temple Prayer Line Lifeline

Prayer Warriors

Chapter Six:

The Faith

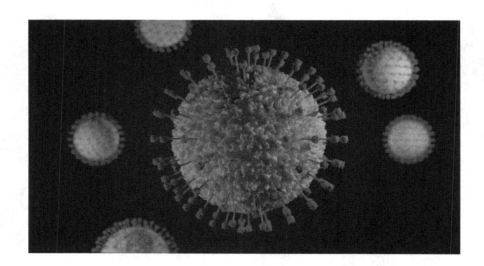

T he day before I was placed on the ventilator was one of the worst days I had experienced. My oxygen levels dropped to an all-time low. The nurses tried everything they knew to do: breathing treatments, different masks, and even turning the oxygen dial all the way up. Nothing worked for me.

Darryl never stopped believing in God, nor did he give up. He kept the faith and began to trust God, our Righteous Healer, even more. Remember when I told you he spoke with authority while walking the floor all night? He would say, "God, if I have to walk this floor all night, Lord, praying to You until my knees break or this floor breaks, I need You to come into this room and show up and show out. Work a miracle for my wife." He asked God to breathe into my lungs so that my level would stay at a normal percentage. Within minutes of that prayer, God showed up again. My oxygen level began to change immediately, from 72 to a healthy 97—and it remained that way throughout the night into the next morning. To God be the glory!

How many of you know that if you call on Jesus, He will answer you?

So many times, we had to walk by faith while in that hospital. The enemy tried to shake my faith, though.

I remember when the nurses removed the breathing tube from my windpipe and exchanged it for a face mask so that I could breathe. One day, a nurse came to check my vitals, and I heard her talking to my husband, explaining to him what was going on with me, but I did not understand what she was saying to him. I was curious, so I asked, "What happened?" She looked at me and shook her head from side to side, meaning 'nothing happened.' When I asked her to tell me the truth, she explained the ventilator was breathing 80% for me and that I was only breathing 20% on my own. All I did was close my eyes and pray to my Righteous Healer, asking Him to breathe His air into my body, for He was the One who made me. He is the Potter, and I am the clay. The Potter knows how to put the clay back together again.

After I prayed to God, the Spirit of Peace came over me. I felt His presence in the room. I kept the faith, no matter what my ears heard, because faith comes by hearing, and hearing by the Word of God (Romans 10:17).(KJV)

Each day, the percentage of me breathing on my own increased, slowly but surely. I was told if I maintained a minimum of 40% usage of the ventilator and 60% of me breathing on my own, they would remove me completely off the machine. I was overjoyed! That was good news to my ears! Within one week, I was able to breathe without the machine. I recall talking all day long that day. However, as a result, the next day, my oxygen level suddenly crashed, leaving me unable to utter a word.

Every time something good would happen, it was as if something else would go wrong. Nevertheless, Darryl and I kept the faith because it is faith that moves God.

The pulmonologist ordered a CPAP mask, which forced a large amount of air into my lungs, enabling me to breathe without the use of the ventilator. I felt like the CPAP mask did more harm than good to the inside of my throat, mouth, tongue, and lips. What a nightmare! Although a lot of air was forced down my windpipe, I still felt as if I couldn't breathe. Darryl said I really looked as if I was suffering and in pain while wearing that mask and felt really bad for me.

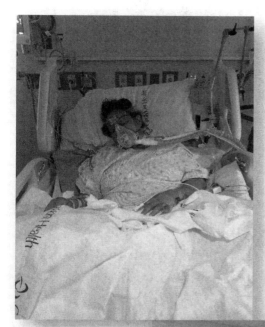

Vickie wearing the CPAP mask.

Selfie of Darryl Hall, Sr.

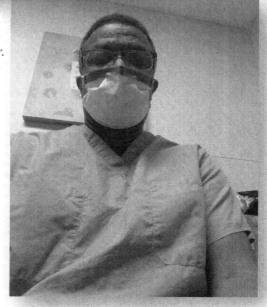

From the beginning to the end, Darryl and I went into the hospital on faith. We then got together with faith and came out by faith because we know faith is the substance of things hoped for and the evidence of things not seen.

When I was in the process of recovering, I realized it was no longer about Darryl or me; it was all about submitting to the will of God. We had the opportunity to pray for some of the medical professionals during my stay. Despite the pandemic, they continued to come to work, standing on the front line for all of God's people, even though their lives were at risk. They could have stayed home with their families and not come in at all. Some were afraid to return home and risk putting their families in danger. Still, they kept coming by faith and kept working through faith because faith without works is dead. Faith is not something we see with our eyes. Rather, it is something that we know, having the assurance and the confidence that it shall come to pass. After we prayed with some of the medical professionals, we bore witness to how their countenance changed. Peace came over them, even while tears flowed from their eyes. They gave us thanks, but Darryl and I gave all the glory to God because He deserves it.

We must always keep on the Shield of Faith through all of our trials and tests in this world today. God's promises are Yes and Amen. To everyone reading this book, I want to encourage you:

Whatever you are going through, hold on to God's unfailing hand.

Keep the faith always, through:

- ❖ Sickness
- ❖ Disease
- ❖ Stress
- ❖ Hurt
- ❖ Depression
- ❖ Provision
- ❖ Heartache
- ❖ Death
- ❖ Hardship
- ❖ Loneliness
- ❖ Anxiety
- ❖ Suicidal thoughts
- ❖ Confusion
- ❖ Broken hearts
- ❖ Disappointments
- ❖ Separation
- ❖ Every attack from the enemy

God can deliver you from them ALL because He is God! I didn't tell you that by hearsay; I share with you from experience. Continue to speak God's Word over whatever the situation.

As you continue reading this book, you will understand more and more about what God did for me. Sometimes, we try to use all other remedies and methods or attempt to come up with our own solutions.

How many of you know we can always call on the name of:

- ❖ Jehovah Jireh—The Lord Our Provider (Genesis 22:14) (NIV)
- ❖ Jehovah Rapha—The Lord Our Healer (Exodus 15:26) (NIV)
- ❖ Jehovah Nissi—The Lord Our Banner (Exodus 17:15) (NIV)
- ❖ Jehovah Shammah—The Lord Is There (Ezekiel 48:35) (NIV)
- ❖ Jehovah Shalom—The Lord Our Peace (Judges 6:24) (NIV)
- ❖ Jehovah Raah—The Lord Our Shepherd (Ezekiel 34:11-12)(NIV)
- ❖ Jehovah El-Shaddai—The Lord God Almighty (Genesis 17:1)(NIV)
- ❖ Jehovah Tsidkenu—The Lord Our Righteousness (Jeremiah 23:5-6)(NIV)

Chapter Seven:

The Miracles

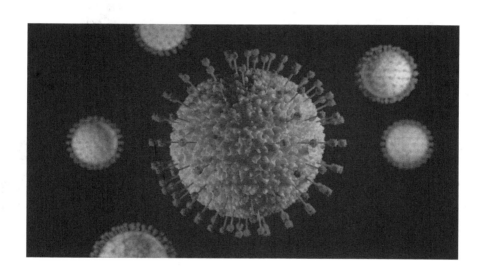

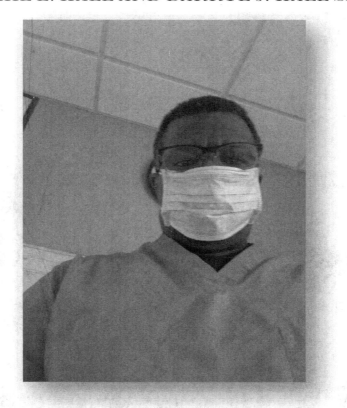

Selfie of Darryl Hall, Sr. Image 13

As I've stated, God was with Darryl and me from the beginning of this life-changing ordeal. However, Before I dive deeply into this chapter, let's do a recap of the miracles that occurred early on:

❖ In Chapter One, God spoke to my husband, instructing him to come upstairs, where he discovered me near death.

❖ In Chapter Two, Darryl and I were placed in isolation together. He was able to take care of me, bathe me, and kiss on me daily—all while I was infected with COVID-19, yet he did not contract the virus.

- ❖ In Chapter Three, God allowed favor with the hospital's Administrator, who went against their visitation policy AND the CDC's guidelines. Darryl was able to be there by my side for the entirety of my hospital stay: 30 days.
- ❖ In Chapter Four, my husband was speaking with the doctor about not putting me on a ventilator (per my wishes). While I was asleep, God dealt with me concerning being placed on the machine. I suddenly opened my eyes and asked to be placed on the ventilator.
- ❖ In Chapter Five, the Prayer Warriors prayed and asked God to show up. He answered every prayer, and prophecies concerning my life came to pass.
- ❖ In Chapter Six, on several occasions when prayer was made by faith, it took ten minutes or less for God to show up and show out.

****

Now that you're all caught up and refreshed, let me share with you the main reason for this particular chapter.

After my first day on the ventilator, my husband told me all my vital signs and bodily functions began to fail. I was literally dying before his eyes. He explained to me how the nurses were running around, checking to make sure they had done everything possible to keep me alive. He said he just sat down and started praying within himself, all while being very watchful of what was going on around me and to me.

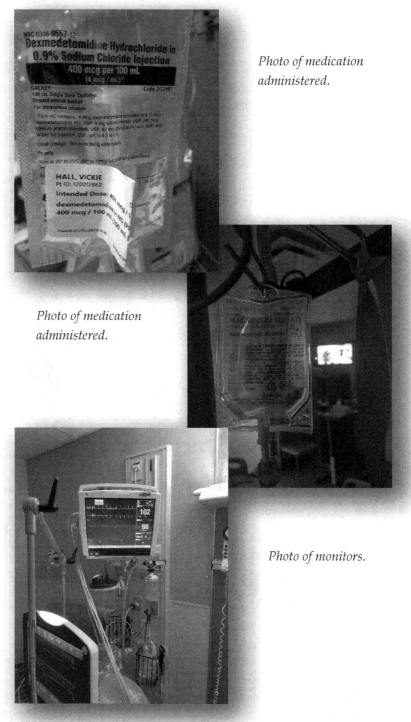

Photo of medication administered.

Photo of medication administered.

Photo of monitors.

JESUS OUR RIGHTEOUS HEALER

At one point, some nurses exited the room to get some other life-saving devices. Another nurse called for the doctor because I was not responding to treatment. During that time, Darryl said he noticed me raising my arms, and he told the nurses to look at me. When they did, the monitors indicated I was still in a coma and non-responsive. He went on to say to me I continued to raise both arms and then suddenly motioned with my hands for him to come to my bedside. He told the nurse, "She's calling me to her."

"I think she is!" replied the stunned nurse.

Once at my side, he said he leaned over and spoke in my ear, "I'm still here." In response to his voice of comfort and assurance, I began using hand motions, which, during that time, both were wearing protective mitts. At first, he thought I was asking him to pray because I had placed my hands together in a praying hands position. However, when he asked me if I wanted him to pray, I shook my head no. He said I then turned my hands sideways and rubbed them together. Immediately, he thought of the childhood game, Rock-Scissor-Paper. He asked if I wanted paper, and I shook my head, motioning yes.

The nurse standing next to him asked another nurse in the room to get me paper and a pen. When she returned, Darryl was asked if I was right- or left-handed. "She's left-handed." The nurse removed my left mitt. My husband then placed the paper on a magazine, while the nurse put the pen in my left hand.

Darryl held the paper in front of me as I began to write, and he spoke aloud what I was writing. He said I wrote the letter 'I.' Then, while writing the next letter, the pen slipped a little, causing the 'C' in 'CAN'T,' which was the next word, to be a bit deformed. The next thing I wrote was a letter 'B,' and then I paused, moving my hand upward, causing a space with the next set of letters that spelled 'BREATHE.' I moved the pen downward, drawing a line to the next words: 'YOU || LL NEED TO,' which he said he spoke, "You all need to..." I moved the pen to the next line, pausing to make a small line, before writing 'PULL ME UP.' The next thing I wrote rather quickly: 'OUT OF THIS,' which appeared kind of jumbled up, but he managed to decipher it just as it was written.

Darryl then told me what amazed him next was how I moved the pen down slightly and drew some sort of angle diagram, as if I were connecting the dots. He said I moved the pen down and wrote 'POSITION.' After that, he said I wrote 'ASAP' with authority.

The nurse asked my husband to help pull me upward in the bed, thinking that would help me breathe better. After they repositioned me, Darryl asked me if I could breathe better. In response, he said I motioned my head, waved my hand, and moved my finger side to side, indicating "No."

Darryl said he and the nurse looked at the machines, while the nurse asked, "How can this be? She is in a coma." At that point, the nurse took the paper I had written on, looked it over, and told my husband she thought he was correct about what he had read aloud. Still, she kept asking, "How could this be?" Shortly after, the rest of the medical team returned and started working on me again.

Photo of medication administered.

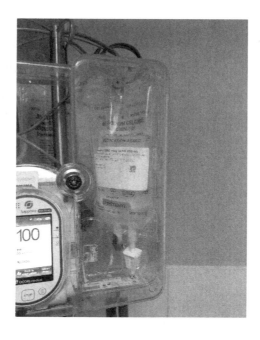

Photo of medication administered. Image 18

He told me he asked the nurse for the paper and then folded it, placing it in my Bible before sitting down again. As he watched the activity going on around me, he continued to pray within himself.

The nurses kept asking, "Where is the doctor?" After about ten minutes or so, Darryl told me a tall doctor walked into the room. He paused at the door as he listened to the nurses tell him about all the medicines and procedures they had tried that didn't work. My husband said the doctor looked at him and asked how he was doing and assured him he was going to take care of me. Darryl watched the doctor as he stood at the door with his hands crossed in front of his body, never moving from that spot but listening to the nurses' chatter.

Suddenly, the doctor said, "You all have to change her position." Darryl said he snapped his head around and looked at the doctor in disbelief because the doctor was not there when I had written the instructions earlier, no one had spoken to him about it, and he hadn't seen the note. (Remember, my husband folded it and placed it in my Bible for safekeeping.)

Darryl explained to me how the nurses looked at the doctor strangely before he said again, "You all have to change her position. Flip her over, pronto! Remove everything on her chest and put it on her back"—meaning all the monitoring and medical devices that were attached to my body. Once they repositioned everything, you won't believe what happened. My husband said ALL the alarms and different sounds that were emitting from the machines, including the ventilator, stopped sounding off. Everything, including my vitals, came under subjection. Within himself, Darryl thought, "My God! The doctor walked in and spoke the exact words my wife wrote, and everything was, indeed, alright."

When the doctor looked at my husband again, he said, "She's okay now. You can take it easy."

"Thank you, and God bless you, doctor."

Darryl also told me that after I was removed from the ventilator, days later and recovering, he never saw the nurse again who had witnessed the miracle with him—although she had been there many days before, caring for me.

As we Prayer Warriors have often said on the prayer line, "Thank you, Jesus, for the miracles, signs, and wonders!"

You are going to be told about other prophecies and miracles further on in this book that continually occurred as God showed up and showed out!

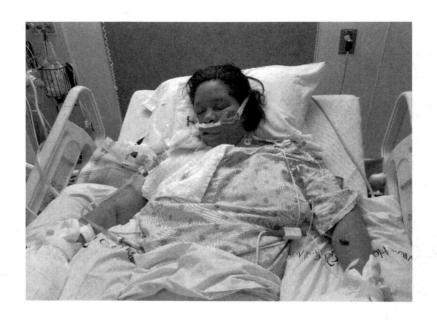

Vickie prior to the miracle when God allowed her to write
instructions to the medical staff while she was in a coma.
(Photo taken by husband, Darryl Hall, Sr.)

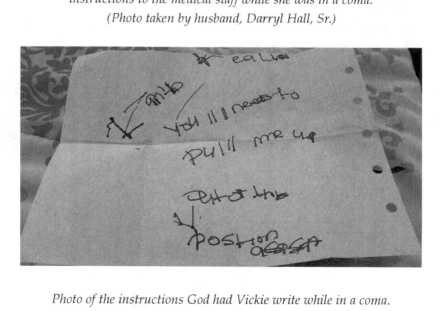

Photo of the instructions God had Vickie write while in a coma.
(Photograph taken by Darryl Hall, Sr.)

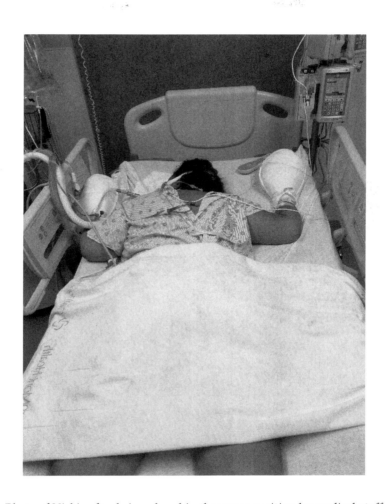

Photo of Vickie after being placed in the prone position by medical staff.
(Photo taken by Darryl Hall, Sr.)

Chapter Eight:

The Fight

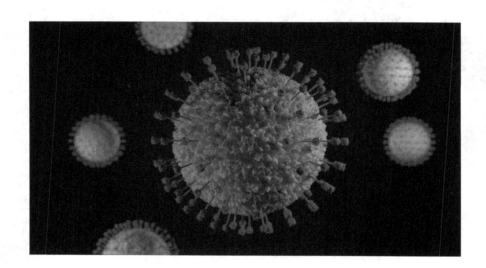

C oming up as a child, I was a fighter by nature. You see, I was raised in the inner-city of Miami, Florida, where the old cliché "survival of the fittest" was my reality. However, when God came into my life, He changed me. What in the world meant for bad, God turned it around for my good. I no longer have to fight in a "bad" way. Instead, I fight the good fight of faith because the battle is not mine; it's the Lord's.

The day I felt my life slipping away, and Darryl discovered me upstairs in the bed, he raised me and spoke life in my ear. At that time, I fought to come back.

Several times, while in the hospital, when my lungs were tired and I desperately gasped for air, God's Word and my great faith inspired me to continue fighting for my life. I'm grateful for how God moved in a very special way. Having my husband right there to speak encouraging words in my ear to increase the intensity of that fight for survival.

"Wherefore, take unto you the whole armour of God, that ye may be able to withstand in the evil day, and having done all, to stand."
~ Ephesians 6:13 ~(KJV)

Darryl told me that even while I was on the ventilator, he knew I never stopped fighting for my life. I experienced high fevers, my vitals were failing, and COVID-19 ravaged my body, yet through all the storm, I fought the fight. My husband received calls from God's people and the Prayer Warriors who told him I was going to live and not die, God was going to raise me up, and that he was to read Psalm 91 over me daily.

Spiritual warfare and the attacks we endure are serious, but Scripture reminds us in Ephesians 6:12 (KJV)

"For we wrestle not against flesh and blood, but against principalities, against powers, against the rulers of the darkness of this world, against spiritual wickedness in high places."

An Apostle from Louisiana called and told Darryl to be strong and that God said I was with Him but that He would not be keeping me; I would be returned after my visit. The Apostle also left a prayer for Darryl to pray over me until I returned. I share it here:

Father, in the Mighty, Glorious, and Most Powerful Name of Jesus Christ,

I command every joint, bone, organ, and tissue to line up to Your will for my wife's life, in Jesus' Name. I declare a supernatural manifestation of Your glory to be revealed in the power of Your resurrection of my wife from this infirmity and demonic plan of Satan. I declare the angels will safely transport her from the heavens back into the shell You've tabernacle her spirit to dwell in, without any backlash from the devil. I command the angels of Heaven to ascend and descend now! I declare total supernatural healing from the top of her head to the soles of her feet! I declare she will preach with double-power and with a double-anointing after this, in Jesus' Name! I call her forth now in power, now in strength, and now in wholeness, in Jesus' Name. I declare it is so!

Amen.

~~~~~~~~~~

After awakening from my coma, my husband reminded me of the many days I did not eat. He often told me that without nourishment, I would not be able to sustain life. I had not eaten for weeks, I lost a substantial amount of weight, and I was in a weakened state as the Coronavirus ravaged my human existence. Still, through it all, I continued to fight.

Although I was awake, I remained on the ventilator—and fought to live.

When I was removed from the ventilator, I fought to breathe.

After speech therapy, I fought to communicate so that I could talk again.

When the time came for me to consume solid foods again, I fought to eat.

When it was time for physical therapy, I fought to walk and perform basic life skills.

To sum it up, without food, without a voice, without fine motor skills, but with the will to live, I closed my eyes and meditated on God—which was enough to keep me in the fight! Even after being released from the hospital and Coronavirus-free, I still must fight. The doctors told me it would take six to nine months to recover fully.

I am a fighter! I am going to fight to the end because I am

worth fighting for, and God has the final say over my life. When the enemy sticks his ugly head up, I am reminded:

"Submit yourselves, therefore, to God.
Resist the devil, and he will flee from you."
~ James 4:7 ~(KJV)

Chapter Nine:

The Visitation

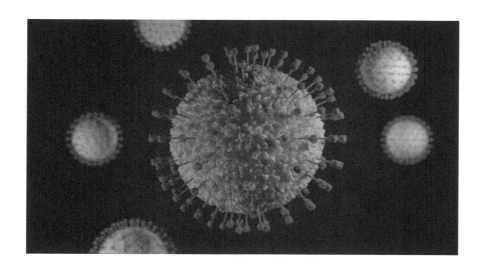

Accepting Jesus Christ as my personal Lord and Savior and surrendering my life to God was one of the greatest resolutions I've ever made. I wanted to get to know Him and who He is for myself, so I began falling in love with Him. It was like love at first sight.

I often wondered what Heaven looked like and would ask God if I could have just a glimpse. He may not come when we want Him, but He will surely come whenever we need Him!

How many of you know we must be very careful about what we ask God for?

For those who don't know, allow me to share with you that the number seven represents perfection and completeness. It's representative of God's creation of all things (see Genesis 1:1, 21-27; 2:3-4).(KJV)

God is so awesome! Let me tell you what He did:

During my ordeal, I had seven visitations, which brings me to the reason why I am writing this chapter. My first visitation with God was when I was asleep in the hospital. He showed me in a dream that I needed to get on a ventilator. (Remember, before that time, I told my husband I never wanted to be placed on one.) As a result of my obedience to God, I am alive today.

My second visitation, I imagine God remembered me asking Him if I could get just a glimpse of Heaven. While in the coma, I experienced a significant, divine visitation with God. I saw a big, beautiful chariot floating in the sky, with bright, sparkling lights that shined like crystal. When I looked up towards the sky, there appeared to be a woman in the image of my grandmother, whom God had called home. She was sitting on the inside of the chariot. I now understand the meaning of 2 Corinthians 5:6-8 (KJV) that states:

"So, we are always confident knowing that while we are at home in the body, we are absent from the Lord. For we walk by faith, not by sight. We are confident, yes, well pleased, rather to be absent from the body and to be present with the Lord."

There was a long silver pole I had to climb to reach the top. Once there, I saw my grandmother all dressed up, looking like a beautiful angel. She was in a hurry, though. She asked, "Vickie, are you coming?" As I clung to the pole, I was undecided: Should I go with her or return? I replied, "No. I must go back and set thine house in order." I knew I had family members that needed salvation, and my work on earth was not finished. Immediately after I spoke those words to her, she took off like a mighty wind, riding in the chariot.

As I began to make my way down the pole, I heard a loud voice from Heaven call out my name. "Vickie!" When I heard the powerful voice, I immediately stopped and looked up. God spoke the following words to me:

"I don't have an ought against you. Your name has been written down in the Book of Life."

I then made my way all the way down the pole. In the supernatural power of God, I was transitioned back to life here on earth. I know God is real. He is not dead; He is alive and has all power in His hands.

As I came to myself, God allowed my eyes to open, but everything was blurry. I really didn't understand what was going on, but I remained calm and humble. When my eyes started to close again, He revealed to me a big field with dark green grass. The texture of the grass was unlike anything here on earth. As I walked through the field, God ministered to me. As tears fell from my eyes, all I could do was give God praise and worship Him in spirit and truth.

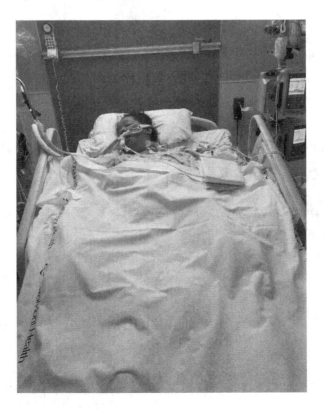

Vickie placed on her back four days after being prone.
(Photo taken by Darryl Hall, Sr.) Image 22

The next time I opened my eyes, I saw my husband standing by my side. He never left me. I truly thank God for him and how He joined us together as one flesh—a union on which He set His approval.

My third visitation was when I was sitting up in a chair, thinking about everything I was going through in the hospital. I felt very vulnerable, and my body was frail. To be honest, I really didn't want anyone else to touch me at all, due to the ridiculous number of injections the nurses had to administer to me. I was tired of it. Each time I had to have blood drawn, it felt like a nightmare that was never going to end. It was difficult for the nurses to draw blood because my veins had collapsed from dehydration and all the medications I was taking. All I wanted to do was rest.

How many of you know that when you are in the hospital, that is the last place you will get rest? (Haha!)

Amidst all that I was going through, I heard the voice of God say, "Go through, daughter." After hearing those words, the peace of God came over me—the peace of God, which passeth all understanding. I knew He was with me because He promised never to leave nor forsake me. God is so amazing!

I must note here that even after I was treated for COVID-19 and released from the hospital, the doctors still wanted Darryl and me to be retested once we returned to our home state. You see, the enemy will bring doubt to your mind if you don't keep the faith and know within your heart that God is a healer.

My fourth visitation with God was when I was a little bit worried about whether I was still positive with the virus or not. What if my husband contracted it from me? God already knew what I was thinking. After all, He's GOD! He knows EVERYTHING!

Within seconds of those thoughts crossing my mind, God spoke in a small, still voice and said, "You don't have Coronavirus. Neither does your husband." When I heard Him speak, I looked around to make sure I was not hallucinating because of all the medication I had been treated with. God then repeated Himself a second time a little louder. I replied, "Thank you, Jesus." However, I didn't say it as if I had the confidence and believed what He said. The last time He spoke, He did so with power and might. At that moment, I felt God's presence all over me.

It doesn't matter how long we've been saved; there are times we will face trials and tribulations that we won't know how we are going to make it through. I've learned (and am still learning) how to lean and depend on God.

My fifth visitation with God was when I was wondering, "How will I be able to live with my health like this on a daily basis, knowing I had a long road to recovery?" As I was meditating on the Lord, He spoke to me, saying, "I am going to give you a full recovery." I laughed within myself because God was showing me that from the beginning, He had been there all the time.

God is Omniscient. He knows all things in our past, present, and future, long before we do. He is the Beginning and the End.

The sixth visitation with God was when I was still in the hospital. He put in my spirit to write a book. I shared with Darryl what God said, and he looked at me and smiled. Well, unbeknownst to me, my husband had been photographically documenting the whole ordeal through all phases and progressions of my recovery—totally unaware that I would need those photographs for this book. God put His stamp of approval on it all. I believe He wanted me to write my testimony so that everyone who reads it will see the following:

- ❖ God is real.
- ❖ He is still in the healing business.
- ❖ He is the same God of yesterday, today, and forever more.
- ❖ He changes not.
- ❖ He has no respect of person.
- ❖ He is our Righteous Healer for the whole world of today and forever more.

I am one of God's living testimonies. Even when I was on my deathbed, God breathed LIFE back into my body. He is truly a miracle worker.

The seventh visitation represents the completion of everything God spoke. He confirmed and manifested it all. He also reminded me about when I was in a coma, and it was He who had me write His instructions on the paper for the medical professionals to change my position—something that ultimately saved my life.

Chapter Ten:

The Restoration

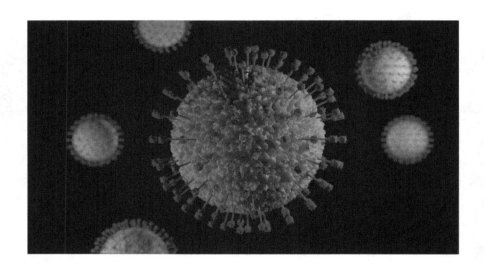

JESUS OUR RIGHTEOUS HEALER

In March 2020, the doctors decided to have me removed from the ventilator after being connected to it for approximately eight days. That was a miracle within itself, as the average minimum time to be connected to that machine is 15 days. The number eight is incredibly significant because it represents **Resurrection** and **Regeneration**. My husband stated he was told that after 15 days, the doctors would reevaluate my situation because I was in such bad shape.

As I think on the goodness of the Lord and all that He has done for me, my soul cries out, "HALLELUJAH!" God can do the miraculous. Only His divine, supernatural power could have restored me. Not only did He restore half of me, He restored ALL of me—my heart, mind, body, and soul. That is why I call Him my Righteous Healer!

"Let us know the Lord will sustain him on his sickbed;
in his illness, you restore him to full health."
~ Psalm 43:3 ~(NASV)

As I laid in the bed, my body was weak, but, according to the doctors, my heart was very strong. My vital signs had maintained a somewhat stable level, at least enough for me to come off the ventilator. My oxygen percentage was sustainable, as well. Through it all, I knew God was with me. Step by step and day by day, it was a growing process. Meanwhile, I could still feel the breathing tube down my throat, the feeding tube in my stomach, and the picc line inside my neck.

Keep in mind that while I was on the ventilator, even though it was assisting my respiratory deficiency, it was proving harmful to my brain. I suffered some form of physical and mental impairment while attached to that machine. Physically, I had to learn how to talk, walk, sit, stand, eat, and swallow again after being removed. Mentally, I was depressed and ashamed.

You never realize how important it is to have the use and activity of all your limbs working perfectly on your body until your experience that lack for yourself. As for me, I felt like a newborn baby when I had to start all over again.

I thank God for being gracious to me and for how He restored me to good health.

"Beloved, I wish above all things that thou mayest prosper and be in health, even as thy soul prospereth."
~ 3 John 1:2 ~(KJV)

The process of recovery took a lot of patience. It was not something that could be accomplished overnight. A lot of times, I was overwhelmed and frustrated, but I did not give up. I kept believing God was going to heal and deliver me from that horrific disease, in the Name of Jesus.

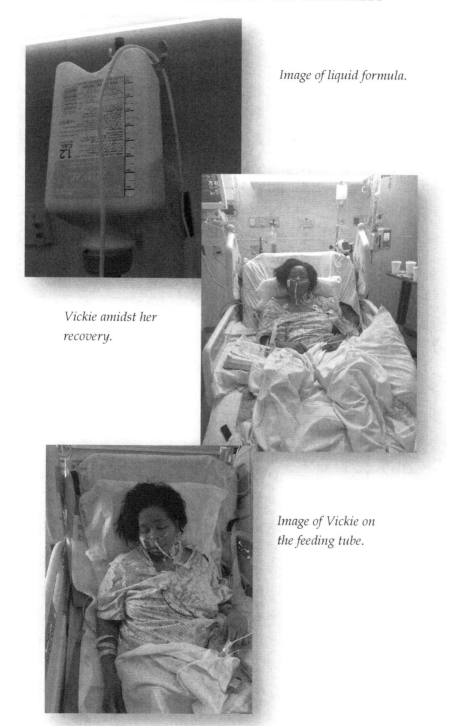

Image of liquid formula.

Vickie amidst her recovery.

Image of Vickie on the feeding tube.

As time progressed, I felt my appetite returning but knew I was still unable to eat. One day, the nurse came to do her daily routine of checking my vitals and making sure that everything was functioning correctly. I decided to use my hands to get her attention, letting her know I was very hungry. I couldn't talk at the time and was unable to eat from the time spent on the ventilator. She explained to me I was already receiving food through the feeding tube and that once the doctor gave his approval, they would remove the tube.

They continued to monitor my vitals daily, with each day getting better for me. The doctor told Darryl that in a few days, they would remove the feeding tube once I reached a certain percentage. Unfortunately, when that day came, nothing happened. I was very disappointed, but the doctors wanted to make sure I was ready and wouldn't have any complications.

When the nurses returned the following day, my husband reminded them about what the doctors said regarding removing the tube, and they did it. That was a big relief. My mouth was very dry, and the skin on my outer lips was extremely cracked. I remember trying to talk to Darryl, and my lips moved up and down, but I was unable to formulate words or sounds. He looked at me, smiled, and said, "I don't understand a word you are saying, Baby." I thought I could communicate with him by writing on paper, but my hands weren't strong enough to form the letters into a sentence because the reflexes in my hand were very weak. I was upset and aggravated. Nevertheless, my husband continued to encourage me, letting me know that in due season, everything was going to be alright.

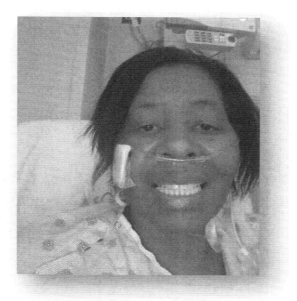

Image of Vickie's lips healing.
(Photo taken by Darryl Hall, Sr.)

The nurses assigned to me were very nice and practiced so much patience with me. All I could say within myself was, "Thank you, Jesus." God surely placed the right people on my path to care for me.

Message: When you treat people right, righteous must return to you. That's why it's good to sow good seeds. When it's time to reap, you can reap good seeds.

When the nurses removed the feeding tube, I knew restoration was taking place in my body. I thought once the tube was removed, I could eat some solid food (I was famished and ready for some sense of normalcy). The speech therapist came to see me to establish a schedule of assisting me with learning how to speak again and to train me how to swallow without choking. The first thing I was permitted to "eat" was crushed ice. They monitored me each time, ensuring I did not choke on the ice. That was repeated time and time again. The speech therapist asked me to cough. At the time, my vocal cords weren't ready for that task. My voice was still shallow, significantly reducing my ability to speak, let alone forcibly cough.

Darryl, the Prayer Warriors, and others uplifted me, and within two days, God had touched my voice, enabling me to talk again. I verbally communicated with my husband, my family on the telephone, and the medical staff.

It was then that Darryl told me about what I had written down while in the coma. I could not believe all that he told me, but when he removed the paper from my Bible and showed me, I knew only God could have performed that miracle. It was truly miraculous because when I attempted to write in the natural, I was unable to.

How many of you know that when you are thinking one way, God will blow your mind when He shows you His way?

God is the way…the ONLY way!

"'My thoughts are not your thoughts,
neither are your ways My ways,' saith the Lord."
~ Isaiah 55:8 ~(KJV)

The staff waited a couple of days before returning because they knew my vocal cords were still very weak, and I needed more time. Imagine the speech therapist's surprise when it was revealed that I could talk without them having to teach me! That time, when I was asked to cough, it came forth much stronger than the days before. When the crushed ice made its appearance again, I swallowed with relative ease and no complications. I suppose it helped that I was still craving real food, coupled with the fact that my mouth was very dry. For three days in a row, they repeated the process. Once the therapist determined I was capable of swallowing without choking on the ice, I graduated to Jell-O and then to popsicles—a routine that continued for an additional three days.

The glorious day came when the therapist said I was ready to eat soft solid foods…with restrictions. By then, I was hungry enough to eat a horse—literally. I can't forget to mention I was diagnosed with diabetes and high blood pressure. As well, my potassium level was low.

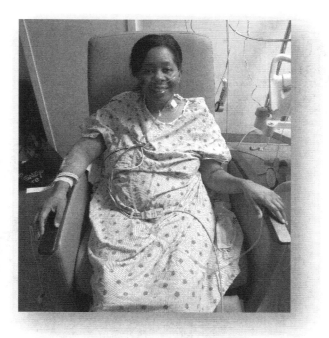

Vickie's smiling face after being approved to eat solid foods.
(Photo taken by Darryl Hall, Sr.)

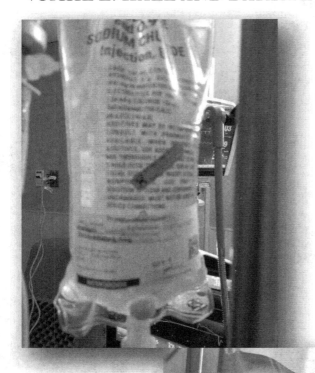

Image of medication administered.

Image of medication administered.

While lying in my bed one day, my body still fragile from being in the same position for an extended period, I was anxious to get up and walk. I told Darryl I needed to use the bathroom, and he said, "Okay. I will call for the nurse to assist you."

"No. Don't call the nurse," I hurriedly said. I felt like I was ready to walk on my own.

How many of you know that whenever you are at your weakest hour, the enemy will show up—first attacking your mind, with all else to follow?

I thank God that from the beginning, God had my head, which is my husband, to be in his righteous position and speak in his authority. My husband let me know that I was not ready to walk on my own.

Sometimes, we may think we are ready for whatever the task at hand when, in reality, we are not.

Obedience is better than sacrifice. Can you imagine if I would have tried to walk on my own? Anything could have happened to me. The enemy already knew what could have taken place because right before the blessing comes, the enemy always shows up. As it pertained to me walking, the physical therapists were coming to provide the full gamut of services so that I could be restored and function while maintaining a healthy life again.

"Submit yourselves, therefore, to God;
resist the devil, and he will flee from you."
~ James 4:7 ~(KJV)

When the physical therapists arrived, so much compassion was shown towards me. They were very pleasant and well-trained. I could feel the love flowing from their hearts. Love, after all, is God's greatest commandment!

"'Master, which is the greatest commandment in the Law? Jesus
said unto him, 'Thou shalt love the Lord thy God with all thy
heart, and with all thy soul, and with all thy mind. This is the
first and great commandment, and the second is like unto it:
Thou shalt love thy neighbor as thyself."
~ Matthew 22:36-39 ~(KJV)

Special Note: A lot of times, when in the hospital, the patient is in a position where they must depend on people they don't know. It's even more challenging when the professionals are dealing with their own issues. Thank God, that wasn't how it was for me.

The first thing the physical therapist asked me to do was sit up with a steady balance on the edge of the bed. My mind was willing, but I didn't have enough strength in my body to sit up on my own. I found myself falling backward in the bed. They helped me get repositioned in the bed, told me to get plenty of rest, and said they would return in two days. I was determined to accomplish the task the next time they came. Why? Because I prayed to my Righteous Healer, asking Him to give me the strength, in the Name of Jesus.

Two days passed, and the therapist returned to reevaluate my strength and range of motion. When I was asked if I could sit up in the bed without falling backward, I did so—without any help! I was then asked if I could move my legs from side to side, which I did as well. Both of my legs moved in each direction.

The joy of the Lord is my strength!

They were amazed to see how much I had progressed in two days' time. I was told that on their next visit, they would work with me concerning my flexibility, posture, mobility, and balance

The first time standing after being bedridden for so long was truly a memorable moment. When I attempted to stand, it was complicated because my body was still fragile. After all, I had minimal (at best) movement of my limbs for quite a while. I recall my legs feeling like a ton of Jell-O. No matter how hard I tried, I could not remain upright with a steady balance. Still, I was determined to do it, even if not for a long period of time. Unfortunately, the stress from the pressure I placed upon myself caused my heart rate to elevate past the normal range, and my blood pressure began to rise. As a result, the physical therapist told me to take it easy and that they would work with me one day at a time. After that ordeal, I needed to rest, so the therapist took their leave.

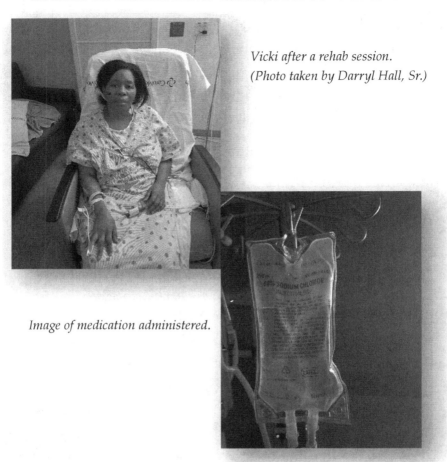

Vicki after a rehab session.
(Photo taken by Darryl Hall, Sr.)

Image of medication administered.

Despite how my body reacted, my trust remained in the Lord. It was prophesied from our Chief Apostle in South Carolina that within the week—three days, to be exact—I would be up and walking.

How many of you know that God is a miracle-worker?

When the physical therapist returned in two days, I was able to walk around with the support of a walker. Remember: Two days before, I could not even stand! I could not believe how God was doing a new thing for me.

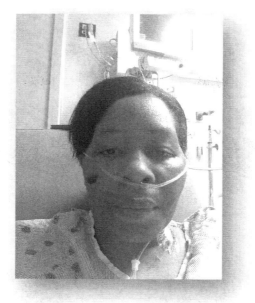

Photo of Vickie during her healing process.
(Photo taken by Darryl Hall, Sr.)

Greater is He that is in me than he that is in the world!

After learning how to walk all over again, that gave me more strength, more faith, and more trust in my Righteous Healer. I will never forget how God spoke to every organ in my body and commanded them to come subject to the Word of God. Whenever and whatever He speaks, it shall come to pass.

"He said, 'Let there be light,' and there was light. God saw the light, that it was good; and God divided the light from the darkness."
~ Genesis 1:3-4 ~(KJV)

Vickie two days before discharge.
(Photo taken by Darryl Hall, Sr.) Image 33

I believe when He spoke to the 12 parts of my inner man (my body), He said, "Let there be LIFE," and then he breathed into my:

1. Circulatory System
2. Integumentary System
3. Skeletal System
4. Muscular System
5. Nervous System
6. Endocrine System
7. Cardiovascular System
8. Lymphatic System
9. Respiratory System
10. Digestive System
11. Urinary System, and
12. Reproductive System

Everything had to connect and line up through obedience. Everything had to fall subject to the Word of God so that I could live and have life, and have it more abundantly, in the Name of Jesus.

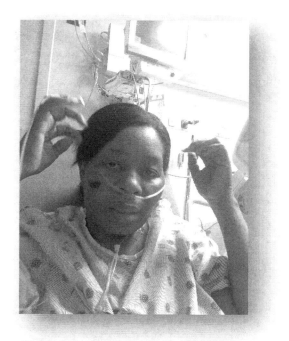

Vickie doing her hair once she was able to.
(Photo taken by Darryl Hall, Sr.) Image 34

What was really amazing to me was one day, Darryl and I were in the room, laughing and talking. Suddenly, people started coming to our room, looking in at the two of us. He said he recognized most of the faces as medical professionals who had taken care of me early on during my stay. (Personally, I did not remember their faces due to my time spent on the ventilator that erased parts of my memory.) Anyway, people were coming out of the woodwork to see me. They were filled with excitement to look upon me. Some mentioned that Darryl and I were "the talk of the town," and they wanted to see for themselves that I had survived. They also commented on how good I looked and that they simply could not believe how well I had recovered. I was, after all, very ill. There were many days they were almost sure I wasn't going to make it. A doctor came in at one point and said that we gave him inspiration and hope, all because of our belief in God. As he spoke, tears formed in his eyes. He said, "I just wanted to see the two of you again," as he shook my husband's hand.

"To God be the glory," we said.

"We need more people in this world like you," the doctor replied.

Darryl turned to look at me and said, "Honey, you are a celebrity! All these people, administrators, doctors, and nurses want to get a glimpse of a living, walking miracle!"

Photo of a smiling Vickie, giving thanks to God for her recovery.
(Photo taken by Darryl Hall, Sr.)

Chapter Eleven:

The Exodus

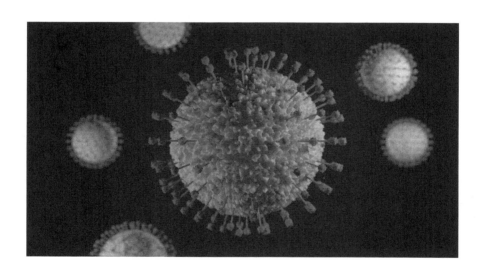

I am forever grateful for how God healed my body from COVID-19. I will shout it out everywhere I go because without Him, my healing would not have taken place. He deserves all the praise, honor, and glory. It ALL belongs to Him.

I'm also thankful for how God instructed the doctors, nurses, and staff, guiding them through every procedure and treatment performed on me.

"For we know that all things work together for the good to them that love God, to them who are called according to His purpose."
~ Romans 8:28 ~(KJV)

The day before I was discharged from the hospital, I remember asking my husband if he could move the chair that I was sitting in and place it by the window. After being there for so long, it felt as if we had been imprisoned due to our isolation. After moving my chair, he then pulled his chair next to mine. We sat together, looking out at God's sunshine and the big, beautiful clouds in the sky. All I could do at that moment was smile and give God praise. My heart was filled with so much joy because the joy of the Lord is my strength!

Sometimes, when we are going through trials and face hardships, it seems like we can't find our way out. However, I'm reminded that Jesus said, "I am the Way, the Truth, and the Life. No one comes to the Father except through Me" (John 14:6).(KJV)

That same day, Darryl and I rejoiced together, waiting for the big day to come. Soon and very soon, we could get out of there and go home. When night fell, I told my husband I was not going to sleep. In fact, there was a clock on the wall that I was determined to watch all night and into the next morning, counting down the time. I'll tell you this: That was some type of experience! My eyes often grew very heavy, and I would doze off for 30 minutes before waking right back up to watch the hands on the clock go around and around.

While sitting there, I suddenly became very impatient. I could feel the spirit of depression coming over me. I had to pray that spirit out of the room. I then started listening to gospel music from my cell phone and pleading the blood of Jesus over my mind.

~~~~~~~~~~

Oh, yeah. That reminds me…

Remember how I mentioned my husband played gospel music continually, 24 hours a day, seven days a week? I forgot to share what he had told me concerning my response to the music.

Sometimes, while I was in the coma, the Spirit of God used to come over me, and I would be praising my God. The nurses used to say, "She likes the music. Look at her wiggling."

Darryl would reply, "If that's what you call it. I know that's the Holy Ghost moving in and over her body."

~~~~~~~~~~

By the time 6:00 a.m. came, Darryl and I were already dressed, packed up, and ready to be discharged. We know everything has its timing, but we were eager to get out of there! Around 9:00 a.m.,

81

the doctor showed up. I was so happy to see her! She explained to me that I no longer required in-patient care from the hospital and that I could go home. She also told me what to expect during my recovery, the different activities I should avoid, and which ones I should do. I was also instructed to eat the right foods and to use the medical equipment I would need at home to give me full support. She also mentioned I would have to have home care, that I needed to continue taking my medication, and should follow up with my Primary Care Physician.

Darryl and Vickie Hall on discharge day!

Prior to our departure, they requested that Darryl and I be retested for COVID-19. We declined and informed them that we would retest once we return home to Miami. The reason we refused the test in North Carolina was not because of the three- to five-day wait on the results or the 14-day quarantine period. Rather, it was because when I was sitting up in the chair in the hospital, I heard the voice of the Lord speak softly to me, saying, "Vickie, you don't have the Coronavirus. Neither does Darryl." Initially, I doubted what I heard—that was until the voice came through louder and more forceful. I looked up and said, "Thank you, Jesus." I knew within my heart that I was healed. Like I said before, there are times the enemy tried to bring us doubt.

After the doctor explained everything to me, the respiratory doctor was called so that my oxygen levels could be checked. If it was low, I would need to travel with an oxygen tank. When we were finally released, a nurse came with a wheelchair to roll me out because I was too weak to walk a long distance. She pushed me down the hallway…with the oxygen. Still, I couldn't wait to get outside!

Once there, I took in all of God's beautiful creations. I was relieved to finally be out of that hospital. I could feel and see the sun shining brightly, and the trees were swaying back and forth with the wind.

Darryl went to get the car while I waited with the nurses. When he pulled up, they helped me get inside. As we made our way back home to Miami, I felt like a new creature and thanked God for restoring me back to life again.

Chapter Twelve:

The Completion

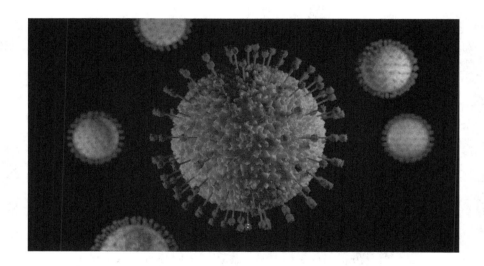

JESUS OUR RIGHTEOUS HEALER

That first day of travel from North Carolina back to Miami, we had to make frequent stops. I needed to rest my legs and feet because I did not want any blood clots to develop in my legs, and I wanted to avoid having my feet swell. During the ride home, my body started feeling very weak. Every time we stopped for a break, each of my family members would take turns helping me get in and out of the car. They assisted me to rest area restrooms and supported me while I was stretching my legs, walking around with the use of a walker with the oxygen tank in tow. Once I made it back to the car and sat down, it felt like all my strength was gone.

Several times during that return trip, the enemy tried to attack my body, but the Prayer Warriors came together on one accord, laid hands on me, and prayed that God would heal my body, all while declaring His Word, in the Name of Jesus. After they prayed for me, I felt so much better.

I thank God for how our family was with us, showing what they do best: Love. That gave me more motivation to press even harder towards my healing destiny.

I also thank God for how our daughter came to support us. Even though she had to take care of our grandchildren, she still made time for me. I am truly blessed beyond measure. We were able to communicate by telephone while I was in the hospital, but I was most grateful for being able to see each other face to face. I recall that whenever I needed certain items or craved a particular food while in the hospital, my daughter and son-in-law would go to the store and purchase everything I needed. There's something to be said when you have a close bond with your children and grandchildren. God is so good! I am thankful for the teachings given to me from my mother that I was able to pass down to my daughter, who can pass it down to her children.

"Train up a child in the way he should go; and when he is old, he will not depart from it."
~ Proverbs 22:6 ~(KJV)

I couldn't wait until Darryl pulled up to the front of our house. Once we arrived, everyone was noticeably exhausted from the long trip, but we were thankful for God's protection as we traveled on those dangerous highways. He did not allow anything to happen to a single hair on our heads.

The front entrance of our home has four stairs leading to the door. Instead of having me walk up them, Darryl pulled into the garage, which afforded me a shorter distance to enter the house. Once inside, I remained on the first floor. The next morning, we got up and went to one of the COVID-19 testing sites to get retested.

The results came back negative for the virus, of course.

Nobody but GOD could have healed my body and shielded my husband through it all, especially after being isolated together in the same room for 30 days!

For the first three days back at home, Darryl and I remained on the first level of the house. I did not have enough strength to make it up the stairs to the second level. I made the best of my temporary "new norm" by using the walker to stand up every now and then. Whenever I had to use the bathroom, my husband would lift me from the chair, place me in the wheelchair, and then push me to the bathroom. At times, I felt as though my situation was becoming impossible to deal with, especially because before I was disabled, I could do for myself without any assistance. I do, however, thank God for how He blessed me with my right rib (my husband). Every time I needed him to help me with anything, he was right there every step of the way.

How many of you know that God knows how to turn your impossible into possible?

"What God has joined together, let no man put asunder."
~ Mark 10:9 ~(KJV)

Each day, my life got better and better. God, Darryl, and my family made very sure of that! Every morning, my mother prepared breakfast for my family and me. Not only did she do that, but she also made sure our family had homecooked meals three times a day. Whatever she could find her hands to do in our house, she fulfilled that role, just like a virtuous mother. I thank God for how He gave my mom the strength and ability to assist my family and me.

I also thank God for my dear brother. Whenever my husband told him I needed certain things from the store, my brother made sure I received it, without hesitation. Before he got off of work, he would always call me to see if I needed anything. Other times, when he was out and about, he would call for the same reason.

We are grateful for our children and grandchildren, too, in the Name of Jesus. To God be the glory!

From the very first day back at home, Darryl never complained. I knew his body was fatigued, yet whenever I had a taste for something special to eat or whatever my heart's desire was, he would go out and bring "it" back.

I had a winning team supporting me 100% and beyond. If we delight ourselves in the Lord, He will give us the desires of our hearts.

Vickie at home, walking with the assistance of her daughter and sister.
(Photo taken by Tamiah Taylor.)

Within one week, I was able to get up and walk. Talk about determination! I cried out to God in prayer, asking Him to heal and deliver me so that I wouldn't have to depend on and be bound to a wheelchair to be transported around. I did not want to have a walker to support me while walking, and I definitely didn't want to contend with being attached to an oxygen tank to assist my respiratory system for the rest of my life.

How many of you know that anything you put your mind to, you can accomplish?

I spoke the Word of God over myself and declared, in the Name of Jesus, that I could do all things through Christ Jesus who gives me strength. God did not bring me this far to leave me in a predicament such as the Coronavirus.

I remember the day as if it were yesterday...

I told Darryl I felt like I was ready to walk upstairs. Although he thought it was too soon, he said, "Okay. If you think you are ready, you can try." While seated in the wheelchair, he pushed me to the base of the stairs. I stood and grabbed hold of the rails. I then turned my body sideways because when I was in the hospital, they trained me on how to go up and down the stairs. I took one step at a time, kept a steady balance, and breathed slowly. My husband stood behind me, making sure I did not fall backward or trip over anything that would cause me to fall. Once I reached the top, Darryl placed the walker in front of me so that I walk from the hallway into our bedroom. I was immensely proud of myself, as that was the farthest I had walked since falling ill.

When I looked around our bedroom, everything was beautiful and ready for me. My body was feeling weak again from walking up the stairs, and I felt myself losing a lot of energy from exerting myself in that way. My oxygen level plummeted to a dangerous low. Darryl then helped me get in bed, making sure I was on oxygen so that I could breathe and raise my level. From that point on, he was very stern with me. I knew once I made it upstairs, he was not going to let me make another move. Therefore, I was on lockdown. (LOL!)

It took a while for me to regain my strength. My husband called the Prayer Warriors, of course so that they could have prayer with me. Once they prayed, strength returned to my body, and I slept like a newborn baby.

The next morning, I was up and ready to take a shower. Darryl was right there willing to assist me, just as he did when we were in the hospital. Fortunately, however, we had more than enough help that time around. Just before he got ready to bathe me, we heard my sister coming up the stairs, making her way into our bathroom. She told my husband she would finish bathing me so that he could get some rest because God knows he needed a whole lot of it. My sister took her time with me and granted me so much patience—not only that day, but every time I needed to bathe. Whenever she was unavailable, she took the time to train my daughter on how to do it.

One day, around noon, I was sitting up in my bed, waiting for my lunch. I saw our grandchildren playing together in the hallway, having so much fun. Seeing them again brought joy to my heart. They came into the room, got up on the bed right beside me, and showered me with kisses and hugs. They had no idea how encouraging that moment was to me. Not being able to see them for 30 days was devastating, heartbreaking, and hurtful for all the family, especially our daughter, who lived right down the street from the hospital.

Although our daughter was unable to visit or see me until I was discharged, God touched my sister's heart to drive all the way to North Carolina (along with my two nieces), so they could be there to comfort our daughter. They helped with our grandchildren and provided other assistance while visiting. Through those tough times, I genuinely appreciated the love and support that was shown to our daughter.

When I woke up the next morning, our daughter came into the room, ready to bathe me and do my hair. I was so happy because my hair really needed to be combed out, washed, and styled. Keep in mind, when I was in the hospital and didn't have enough strength to comb or brush my hair, Darryl combed and styled my hair the best he could with the aid of some lotion. Now, THAT'S love! We are helpers, one to another.

Vickie at home, smiling after her daughter styled her hair.
(Photo taken by Shavondia Jones).

I remember getting out of bed one day, going into the bathroom, and looking at myself in the mirror. Instantly, the tears began to fall, and I could not stop them. The affliction I had to bear in my body shown through. With the help of God abiding down on the inside of me, I went through the fire without getting burned.

"Many are the afflictions of the righteous;
but the Lord delivers him from them all."
~ Psalm 34:19 ~(KJV)

After the doctor had me turned over from my back to my chest while in the hospital, a side-effect of lying face-down (prone) for four days in a coma on the right side of my face was that it caused bruising and immense swelling. It looked like someone had punched me in the face. My left knee and the lower part of my leg were also bruised. The left side of my neck had dark marks from where the picc line had been. The upper part of my body was bruised as well, and my skin was scab-like. I recall my husband stating my body looked like it got ran over by a truck—precisely how I was feeling. The medical professionals who were tending to me overheard Darryl's statement, and they replied, "Even though her body may look really bad because of what she's been through, at least she's still alive."

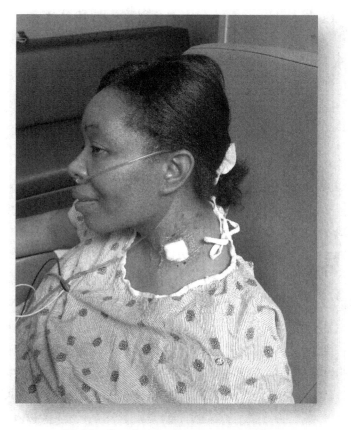

Vickie after the picc line was removed.
(Photo taken by Darryl Hall, Sr.) Image 40

Indeed, by the grace of God alone, I am alive!

You must encourage yourself every chance you get. I did just that—plenty of times.

I knew our family couldn't stay in our home forever. As the days ticked by, it got closer and closer for the time they would depart from us and return to their homes. I count it all joy that they sacrificed their time, lives, and families, just to come to support my husband and me.

After everyone left, I felt kind of sad. Still, life had to go on. I started speaking over myself, saying, "Everything is going to be alright."

One day, Darryl said to me, "Well, Honey, it's just you and me, but we are going to be alright." Those few words proved very encouraging to me.

Can I just speak the truth and be real with you right now?

On many occasions, my husband and I had to run a lot of errands, whether it was going to the store or taking me to doctors' appointments. One day, we were on our way to the store, and he asked me if I was getting out of the car to go with him inside. I told him no. I always made up excuses and stayed in the car, all while knowing in my heart, I wanted to go with him inside. The spirit of shame came upon me. I was concerned about my outer appearance and what others would say or think of me. All types of negative thoughts flowed through my mind. Before I realized it, a spirit of depression came over me. A lot of times, all I could do was cry.

Have you ever heard the expression, "While God is blessing, the enemy is messing"?

Amidst it all, I continued to give God the praise. Even though I knew the Righteous Healer healed my body, my heart and mind needed healing and deliverance, too.

Vickie at home relaxing, sitting in a chair.
(Photo taken by Darryl Hall, Sr.) Image 41

One day, we were on the prayer line with the Prayer Warriors, and it was time for me to testify. When I opened my mouth, I began crying out and telling them how I was really feeling on the inside. At the time, I was facing shame and depression. When the manifestation of the truth came forth, I was free!

"You shall know the truth, and the truth shall make you free."
~ John 8:32 ~(KJV)

The enemy was on the attack, but he had to loose me, in the Name of Jesus!

"Verily, I say unto you; whatsoever ye shall bind on earth, shall be bound in Heaven, and whatsoever you shall loose on earth, shall be loosed in Heaven."
~ Matthew 18:18 ~(KJV)

I had to declare God's Word over my life. I am a survivor because God healed my body. That is not something I read about or heard somewhere; it is something I experienced for myself. I could have lost my life to the Coronavirus, but it is nothing but the blood of Jesus that kept me covered…and alive.

Although this has been a tumultuous journey, I won't complain. My God is SO good! When I was in the hospital and unable to do anything for myself, God spoke to me and said He was going to give me a FULL recovery. I could not see it happening, but I believed it would.

Now that I am home, the road to recovery has been nothing short of miraculous.

- ❖ I can walk without the support of a walker.
- ❖ I no longer need to be pushed around in a wheelchair.
- ❖ I can bathe myself without any assistance from my family.
- ❖ I choose my own clothing and dress myself.
- ❖ I wash and style my hair.
- ❖ I walk up and down the stairs with a steady balance.
- ❖ I can sit up in the bed without falling backward.

❖ I thank God I can breathe all day without the use of oxygen; however, at night, while asleep, I still use the oxygen concentrator to help me breathe. This, too, shall pass, in the Name of Jesus.

❖ I cook my own food, eat, and swallow without choking.

EVERYTHING the enemy stole from me has been restored by God!

For years (before COVID-19), I suffered from varicose veins in the upper part of my legs. I used to be in so much pain and discomfort. When I consulted with a vein specialist to have them removed, I was told that in a few years, they would return. Every chance I had, I laid hands on my legs, anointed them with oil, and prayed to God, asking Him to heal me.

Well, when I was in the hospital being treated for the virus, I was administered all kinds of medication until the day I was discharged. One day, when I was getting out of the shower, I happened to look down at my legs and could not believe what I saw: the varicose veins on my upper thighs were GONE! I gave God the praise and said, "Thank You, Jesus!"

COVID-19 is a deadly and contagious disease that does not discriminate. The virus is ravaging through the land, attacking different ages, races, and ethnicities. It has reached virtually every city, state, and country worldwide. One thing I noticed during my experience is that almost everyone has the same symptoms: double pneumonia in the lungs. Even after being healed from the Coronavirus, the doctors stated that inflammation would be in my lungs for at least six to nine months and will clear up on its own.

The virus brings with it the spirit of division. It causes separation between the Body of Christ, families, and friends from throughout the world. We must take God back to His Word because He is GOD and cannot lie. He is our Righteous Healer.

As of late, we are learning that children of all ages are getting infected with and dying from the virus. Whenever we see plagues dwelling in the land, it's time to pray and really seek the Lord. They are signs of the end of time, and it is near. Cry out to God for our children! That is why God told us not to weep for Him, but weep for ourselves and our children.

I truly believe it is time for the Body of Christ to come together on one accord and with one mind. Let us stand together in unity and love, with prayer and supplication. God has given us the power to spiritually speak life to dead situations and trample the enemy underfoot through His Holy Spirit.

I pray for everyone who is battling COVID-19, that God will heal your body, in the Mighty Name of Jesus.

I decree and declare God's Word over your life, that you shall live and not die, in the Name of Jesus.

I pray for those who have lost loved ones along the way, that God will continue to give you strength, in the Name of Jesus. I plead the blood of Jesus against the principalities, powers, the rulers of the darkness of this world, and against spiritual wickedness in high places, in the Name of Jesus.

I plead the blood of Jesus against the enemy in every form when he comes against our families, children, grandchildren, and finances, in the Name of Jesus.

I speak LIFE over your body and command every part to line up with the Word of God because your body is the temple of God, and the Spirit of God dwelleth in you, in the Name of Jesus.

I speak LIFE to every organ, tissue, cell, and immune system, in the Mighty Name of Jesus.

I speak LIFE to every bone and joint, that they will continue to provide structure for your body, in the Mighty Name of Jesus.

I speak LIFE to every heart and lung, that the blood will continue to pump and flow in every area, from the crown of your head to the very sole of your feet, in the Name of Jesus.

I speak LIFE over our children, that they will obey their parents in the Lord, for this is right. They will honor their father and mother, which is the first commandment with promise, that it may be well with thee, and thou mayest live long on the earth, in the Name of Jesus.

> *"They [Children] are a gift from the Lord;*
> *they are a reward from Him."*
> **~ Psalm 127:3 ~(NITV)**

I speak LIFE over our grandchildren, in the Name of Jesus.

*"They are the crown of the aged,
and the glory of children is their fathers."*
~ Proverbs 17:6 ~(ESV)

I speak LIFE over your finances, that every need shall be met, and that God shall provide.

*"'Bring all the tithes into the storehouse, that there may
be meat in mine house, and prove me now herewith,'
saith the Lord of hosts, 'If I will not open you the
windows of Heaven, and pour you out a blessing, that
there shall not be room enough to receive it.'"*
~ Malachi 3:10 ~(KJV)

I pray for the doctors, nurses, and staff who are working on the front line, that God will continue to cover you all in His blood through this pandemic. God will lead you, guide you, and continue giving you the knowledge to treat all diseases, in the Name of Jesus. I encourage everyone to pray over every medication the doctors have prescribed because prayer changes things.

I truly believe prayer needs to be put back in the schools during this dispensation. When they removed prayer from the schools, everything else found their way in. For everyone who returns to school, I pray for the children, teachers, staff, and administrators, that God will shield, protect, and cover you with His blood, in the Name of Jesus.

I pray for everyone standing on the front line and every law enforcement officer, that God will continue to keep your body safe from harm and danger, in the Name of Jesus.

I pray for everyone sitting in high places and positions, that God will give you compassion, wisdom, knowledge, and understanding to make the correct decisions, in the Name of Jesus.

We need to take Jesus with us everywhere we go and put Him first in our lives. We must stand on God's Word because everything is diminishing, except the Word of God.

> *"Heaven and earth shall pass away,*
> *but My words shall not pass away."*
> **~ Matthew 24:35 ~(KJV)**

As we look around, we can see all that is taking place in the land today—things that were predestinated in God's Word.

> *"And Jesus answered and said unto them, 'Take heed that*
> *no man deceive you. For many shall come in My Name,*
> *saying 'I am Christ,' and shall deceive many. And you shall*
> *hear of wars and rumors of wars: see that ye not be troubled;*
> *for all things must come to pass. But the end is not yet,*
> *for nation shall rise against nation, and kingdom against*
> *kingdom: and there shall be famines, and pestilences, and*
> *earthquakes in divers places. All these are the beginning*
> *of sorrows. For we cannot put our trust in man.'"*
> **~ Matthew 24:4-8 ~(KJV)**

(Psalm 118:8) (KJV) It's better to trust in the Lord, than to put confidence in man. It's not in one nationality, race, religion, or politician. It is in ONE person: Jesus Christ. He is still in charge with all power, majesty, and dominion in His hands. For He is God alone, and besides Him, there is none other.

He is our

Righteous Healer!

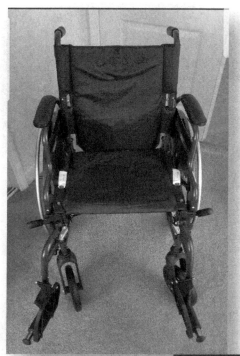

Vickie's wheelchair at home.

Vickie's Oxygen Concentrator.

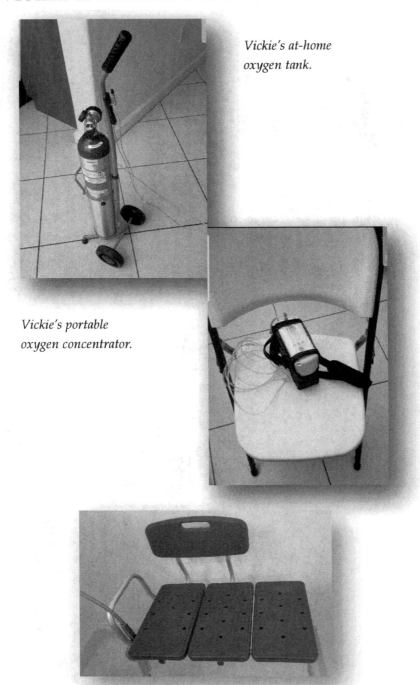

*Vickie's at-home
oxygen tank.*

*Vickie's portable
oxygen concentrator.*

Vickie's shower chair at home.

Final Prayer

Father God, in the Mighty Name of Jesus,

As we come before You in Your presence with a repentant heart, we ask You to forgive us from all of our sins, humbling ourselves at the feet of Jesus. As You sit at the right hand of God, we ask You to intercede for Your people. We are Your people, standing in need of prayer.

God, You said in Your Word, "If My people, which are called by My Name will humble themselves, and pray, seek My face, and turn from their wicked ways, then will I hear from Heaven; and forgive their sins, and I will heal their land" (2 Chronicles 7:14).(KJV)We know our land needs to be healed from this pandemic crisis, Lord. You are the only One who can help and deliver us in times of trouble.

God, Your Name alone is Holy and Powerful, and Your Word is medicine that can heal and cure all sicknesses and diseases in the land. You were wounded for our transgressions and bruised for our iniquities: the chastisement of our peace was upon You; with Your stripes, we are healed (Isaiah 53:5). (KJV)

God, You are the True and Living God. I speak life into every word shared here, through every chapter, every picture, and every prayer contained within this book, that God will seal it with the blood of Jesus.

Amen!

Vickie Hall selfie before her COVID-19 diagnosis.

Vickie Hall after God's Divine healing.
(Photo taken by Darryl Hall, Sr.)